FOREWORD

You'd think that I would know more than most about place-names. It's true that as a weather presenter I've spent a great deal of time looking at maps of Wales decorated with raindrops, hail, ice, snow, and even sunshine – sometimes! I've become well-acquainted with the names given to cities, towns and villages across Wales, and I've often wondered about their origins.

Nothing says more about the history and culture of a place than its name. This lively introduction to the place-names of Wales takes us on a whistle-stop tour, with plenty of entertaining sights to be seen along the way.

Whether you are a native or a tourist, I can guarantee that you will find much to savour here as you learn more about the history of this endlessly fascinating small country. What's in a name? Read on and find out!

Siân Lloyd

INTRODUCTION

Dinefwr Castle

How many times have you come across a place-name in Wales and wondered what it meant? Are you new to Wales and dying to know more about how places came to be called by their current names? If so, this is the book for you!

The place-names of Wales have been the subject of many books, including the *Dictionary of the Place-Names of Wales* by Hywel Wyn Owen and Richard Morgan. Here we take a concise look at the main categories of place-names, exploring some of their meanings and histories. You may speak little or no Welsh, but don't worry, as we explain what names mean and offer a guide to basic pronunciation. We include a list of some of the **elements** in place-names at the end of the book, listed alphabetically for ease of reference. When you come across an element it will always appear in **bold italics**, whereas place-names appear in **bold**.

You'll see that this book explores broad themes, with 'Dictionary Windows' to spotlight definitions. This may whet your appetite for further exploration, in which case the *Dictionary* itself could be your next port of call. We take a look at geographical features such as valleys, mountains and seas before moving on to cover subjects such as castles, holy places and cities, providing basic information about how place-names are 'built'. Place-names are often the subject of myth and local legend that may not be directly responsible for the name itself, despite popular belief. This means you may have one or two surprises when you read on, as things are not always as they seem!

Let us take you on a virtual journey of Wales, via quiet lakes, busy ports and thriving towns.

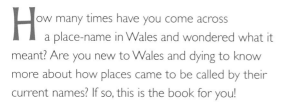

Croeso i enwau lleoedd Cymru . . .

Welcome to the place-names of Wales!

Preface

Ceiriog Valley

We are delighted that Inside Out is getting inside the place-names of Wales. A place-name encapsulates the soul of a place, its history, its landscape, its people, its speech. Understand the place-name, and you'll know the place.

The *Dictionary of the Place-Names of Wales*, which we published in 2007, is an authoritative, scholarly publication that draws together existing knowledge about Wales's place-names. It is the first of its kind, described by one eminent scholar as 'a milestone in the history of Welsh place-name studies'. *Exploring Place-Names in Wales* is based on material in our *Dictionary*, but takes you out of the study and into the byways, towns and villages of Wales, helping you to explore them through their names.

Hywel Wyn Owen, Richard Morgan

Llyn y Foel

How do i pronounce Welsh place-names?

In some ways, Welsh is easier to pronounce than English, partly because Welsh sounds and letters are more consistent. In English we are used to inconsistencies:

- -a- is pronounced differently in 'above', 'fat', 'fate' and 'farm';
- -f- is pronounced differently in 'of' and 'farm';
- -th- differently in 'this' and 'thistle';
- in 'fate' and 'thistle' the -e- is not pronounced any more than the -r- in 'farm'.

In Welsh however:

- -a- is always -a- (as in 'fat');
- -th- is always -th- (as in 'thin');
- -r- is always pronounced.

This link between sounds and letters means that, for example, Welsh uses the letter -dd- as in the sound of 'this', reserving -th- for the sound of 'thistle'. Welsh uses -f- for the sound of the English 'of', and -ff- for the sound of 'farm', in the way that English also distinguishes between English 'of' and 'off'.

Pack your trunk and come to NARBERTH.

A CHECKLIST OF LETTERS AND SOUNDS

Here's a list of letters and sounds you are likely to meet in Welsh place-names. It's not an exhaustive introduction to pronouncing Welsh, so we've omitted sounds like -b-, -m-, -n- and -p-, which are common to most languages.

Welsh letter(s)	comparable English sound	place-name
a	cat	**A**ber
â	car	Pentreg**â**t
e	ten	B**e**tws-y-coed
i	tin	D**i**nas
o	cot	**O**gwen
ô	caught	Tre'r-dd**ô**l
u	if	Al**u**n
w [as a vowel]	good	Bet**w**s-y-coed
ŵ	mood	Tret**ŵ**r
y¹	cut	Betws-**y**-coed
y²	if	Yn**y**s
ŷ	tea	T**ŷ**-croes
c	cat	**C**aerdydd
ch	loch	**Ch**wilog
dd	this	Ffri**dd**
f	of	Llan**f**air
ff	off	**Ff**ridd
g	got	**G**arth
ll	l+h	**Ll**anfair
r	rot	**R**adu**r**
rh	r+h	**Rh**eidol
w [as consonant]	wet	**W**aun-fawr
ae	tie	C**ae**rdydd
au	tie	Caer**au**
ai	tie	Llanf**ai**r
ei	Tay	Rh**ei**dol
eu	Tay	C**eu**nant
ou	toy	Cwm-c**ou**
wy	(French) **oui**	El**wy**
oe	toy	Betws-y-c**oe**d
uw	hue	**Uw**chmynydd

WHERE DOES THE STRESS FALL IN WELSH PLACE-NAMES?

In many English place-names, the stress tends to fall on the first syllable, such as **Bír**mingham and **Glóu**cester, but there are many exceptions, such as Wolver**hámpt**on and Birken**héad**. Welsh tends to stress the penultimate syllable; this applies generally to place-names, no matter how many syllables in the name e.g. **Á**ber, Aber**ý**stwyth, Aberdau**gléd**dau. If in doubt, check for the last syllable but one and stress that one! You might like to call this the 'penultimate stress rule'.

Aberystwyth castle ruins

WATCH OUT FOR THOSE HYPHENS

There are exceptions to the 'penultimate stress rule'. If the last component in the place-name has just one syllable, the place-name is written in such a way that it flags up that the stress, unusually, falls on the single **last syllable**. For example, we say Betws-y-**coed** stressing 'coed' (rather than 'Betwsycoed'). Convention means that we write **Aber-carn** and **Aber-craf** because the river names **Carn** and **Craf** have one syllable and we don't pronounce these places 'Abércarn' and so on. You will find road signs that have been up for decades and haven't been revised to conform to convention, and anglicized versions of place-names tend to go their own way (such as **Abercrave** alongside the Welsh form **Aber-craf**). **The simplest rule is to watch out for hyphens.** They will usually tell you that the stress falls on the **last syllable**.

WHY ARE THERE SO MANY PLACE-NAMES WITH –Y– IN THEM?

-Y- is Welsh for 'the' (the definite article). Some place-names in England have a definite article too, such as **The** Wash, **The** Weald and **The** Downs, and it is commonly used when referring to rivers such as the Mersey and the Thames or areas such as the Lake District.

In Welsh it is far more common. The definite article **-y-** may appear in **Y Bala** and **Y Drenewydd** or in the middle of a word such as **Betws-y-coed**. **Yr** as in **Yr Wyddgrug** precedes a name beginning with a vowel. **-Y-** always sounds like 'uh' or 'cut' at the beginning of a word or when used alone.

A LIGHTNING TOUR OF MUTATIONS

This is a feature of Welsh we won't go into in detail here, and stems from the modification of a consonant in response to a consonant next to it – a neighbour affecting its neighbour if you like! Commonly, the definite article **-y-** can cause this change so that 'y pont newydd' ('the new bridge') becomes **Y Bontnewydd**. In many such instances of place-names, the **-Y-** is now redundant and is just left out: **Bontnewydd**.

The most obvious evidence of mutations you'll see is the fact that *Ilan* affects its following name so that *Ilan Tudno* becomes **Llandudno**, *Ilan Mair* becomes **Llanfair** and *Ilan Cybi* becomes **Llangybi**. The preposition **yn**, 'in', affects the consonant following it too, so that **Llanfair yn Buallt** becomes **Llanfair-ym-Muallt**.

When a -c- becomes a -g- it affects our greeting *Croeso i* **C**ymru which becomes *Croeso i* **G**ymru – Welcome to Wales!

Llandudno

One place, two names –

The long and short of it

Aberteifi (Cardigan)

Names in both English and Welsh for the same place do not always share a meaning; you'll see this later for example with **Abertawe** (**Swansea**). As you travel around Wales you will see that where names have an English version in use, it will be noted on road signs and maps, but in many other cases you will see a Welsh name only as no English version of the name has ever existed. More often than not, dual place-names arose where English settlements developed.

When you find a place with English and Welsh names that bear little correspondence in meaning, for example **Cardigan** – a colloquial use of **Ceredigion**, 'territory of Ceredig', a 5th-century Celtic leader, – and the Welsh **Aberteifi** – 'mouth of the river Teifi' – you can safely put this down to local usage by different groups of people over the years, with both names used concurrently. Since we have mentioned **Cardigan**, now is the time to tell you that this buttoned woolly sweater of the same name was invented by the 7th Earl of Cardigan during the mid-19th century. He was a leader in the Charge of the Light Brigade and his chilly troops were the first to don their 'cardis' during the Crimean War.

The world's longest name?

We cannot explore place-names without reference to what is widely believed to be one of the world's longest names. The train station here bears the incredible sign:

Llanfairpwllgwyngyll gogerychwyrndrobwll- llantysiliogogogoch

But is it really a place-name at all? The official name of the village is **Llanfair Pwllgwyngyll**, used on road signs and maps. It refers to a church overlooking an inlet on the Menai Strait, 'the church of Mair (or Mary) in Pwllgwyngyll'. The township of **Pwllgwyngyll** was the 'pool of white hazel' (**gwyn** and **cyll**) growing in

7th Earl of
Cardigan

the vicinity. The rest of the name is but a fanciful 'add-on' credited to a tailor called Thomas Hughes of Menai Bridge who died in 1890.

When the little temporary railway station at **Llanfair** was about to become redundant in 1850 following completion of the Britannia Bridge (known locally as **Pont Llanfair**), something had to be done to ensure it became a talking-point. The rest of the name was assembled from elements describing the landscape, linked with connecting parts.

LLANFAIR PWLLGWYNGYLL Angl SH5371
'church of Mair in Pwllgwyngyll', *llan*, pers.n. *Mair* (Mary), tnshp n. *Pwllgwyngyll*

Piwllgunyl 1254, *Llan Vair y pwll Gwinghill* 1536-9, *ll. fair ymhwll gwingill* c.1566, *Llanvayrpwllwingill* 1653, *Llanfair-pwllgwyngyll* 1838.

The church overlooks an inlet in the Menai Strait. The popularity of churches called Llanfair necessitated a defining location, in this case the tnshp of Pwllgwyngyll (*Piwllgunyl* 1254, *Pullgwingill* 1543). There is documentary evidence of white hazel (*gwyn*, *coll* pl. *cyll*) in the vicinity. The internationally celebrated addition - gogerychwyrndrobwll-llantysiliogogogoch is little more than a fanciful appendage deliberately coined to ensure continued prominence for a temporary railway station and freight yard about to become redundant following completion in 1850 of the Britannia Bridge (locally Pont Llanfair). A tailor from Menai Bridge (one Thomas Hughes who died in 1890) is credited with the fabrication which is based on features in the immediate landscape. The els are *go* 'somewhat', *ger* 'near', *y* 'the', *chwyrn* 'wild', *trobwll* the 'whirlpool' of Pwll Ceris in the Menai Strait; *Llantysilio* is an allusion to the church of Llandysilio on Ynys Tysilio or Church Island near Menai Bridge, while the tag *-gogogoch* is partly an echo of Llandysiliogogo Card (q.v.) and partly a hint at Ynys Gorad Goch in the Strait.

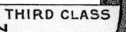

THIRD CLASS — 7725 — L.M.&S.RY. — THIRD CLASS — 7725

LLANRHAIADR-YN-MOCHNANT
TO
LLANFAIRPINWYNGYLLGOGERCHWYNDROBWLLANTYSILIOGOGOG CH. 7725

SOURCE TO ESTUARY –

A LAND OF WATER

Afon Cynfael

Wales is a land carved by water, with abundant rivers, waterfalls and streams. You are never far from it, and place-names make the most of this.

A RIVER'S JOURNEY

As you cross a bridge in Wales, **afon** 'river' sometimes appears on signs along with a river name such as **Afon Glaslyn**. The element **nant** 'stream' denotes the earlier journey of the water, and can also indicate a valley, or valley with a stream running through it. Take **Nant-y-caws** 'river of the cheese', where local legend has it that cheeses were rinsed in the stream centuries ago; in truth the name refers to rich well-watered pasture for dairy cattle. Milk (**llefrith**) appears elsewhere in **Nant Llefrith** and **Afon Llaethnant**, with **llaeth** meaning milk or cream, referring perhaps to the cloudy or milky waters of a stream. A much faster flow is seen in the element **ffrwd,** namely a rapidly flowing stream such as that of **Ffrwd-grech**. Meanwhile **Y Pîl** (**Pyle**) means 'tidal stream'.

The Slebech sword being carried in procession at St Davids Cathedral

A MUDDY MESS OR SLEBECH

Descriptions of watery places take many forms, for example the unusual **Slebech** ('slebetch'). This is still used colloquially in some areas of Pembrokeshire and Ceredigion when people want to describe a mucky mess, and comes directly from the Old English **slǣpe** meaning muddy stream or slippery, marshy place. **Slebech** was just such a spot, and here an old church and site of a hospital of the Knights of St John of Jerusalem lay in an angle between the Eastern **Cleddau** river and an unnamed stream.

Marshy places like fens and bogs often include the element **cors**, such as **Cors Ddyga** (**Malltraeth Marsh**). Dyga or Dygai was an unknown person, as was Mochno, whose land was named **Cors Fochno**.

The dramatically named **Cors Goch Glan Teifi** 'red marsh on Teifi bank' is also known as **Cors Caron** and is near **Tregaron** 'hamlet of Caron'. The marshland's name comes from its red peat, leading to tall tales of blood and corpses in the marsh!

WELLS AND SWIFT WATER

Wherever water runs rapidly place-names reflect this. Names such as **Pistyll Rhaeadr** 'waterfall on the river Rhaeadr' gave rise to a river name, the name of the town of **Rhaeadr** (**Rhayader**) and the description of the rapids. Interestingly **Rhaeadr** also means 'waterfall'.

Springs or wells are shown in the element **ffynnon**, as in **Ffynnongroyw** 'clear well' (**croyw** 'clear'). Water quality was indicated elsewhere such as **Ffynnon Goch**, a 'red spring or well'. **Treffynnon** (**Holywell**) has quite a history.

Dolgoch Falls

HOLYWELL, TREFFYNNON Flints SJ1875 'holy well', 'village of the well', OE *hālig*, OE *wella*, W *tref, ffynnon*

Haliwel 1093, *Haliwell'* 1254, *Halywelle* 1284, *Halywall* 1320, *Holywell* 1465

Treffynnon 1329, *terfynnawn* 1375-80, *trer ffynnon* c.1566, *Holy Well (Wallice Tre ffynnon alias Gwenfrewi)* 1763, *Holywell or Treffynnion* 1813. The legend of Gwenfrewi (anglicized as Winifred) describes her as being beheaded in the 7cent. by a rejected suitor, her head rolling down a hill towards Beuno's chapel with a spring bursting forth where the head came to rest. Beuno, her uncle, restored her head, and a nunnery with Winifred as abbess (*Villa Fontis* 1284, *Llanwenfrewy* 1590) was established around St Winifred's Well (Ffynnon Wenfrewi). The well's curative waters make it a centre of pilgrimage to this day.

St Non's Well

POOLS AND HEADWATERS

Pwll 'pool' and 'pit' is a frequent element in place-names, such as **Pwll-glas** 'verdant pool'. Here a pool in this stream was characterized by the lush foliage surrounding it, and a much larger place shares this element at **Pwllheli** 'brine pool'.

Headwaters are described as **blaen**, as in **Blaenafon** 'head of the river' and **Blaenannerch** 'source of the river Annerch'. Be careful if you see the word **blaenau**, as the plural **-au** makes all the difference and means 'uplands', as in **Blaenau Gwent**.

BRIDGES AND DEVILS

At crossings, place-names with the element **pont** 'bridge' are found. They usually team up with the name of a river such as **Pont-lliw**. You may see a **pont** named after a person such as **Pontfadog** 'Madog's bridge', or after its construction such as **Pontgarreg** 'stone bridge'.

Ponterwyd

Prehistoric bridge over the Cleddau, Llanstinan

One of Wales's most famous bridges is **Devil's Bridge**, bearing the much earlier Welsh name **Pontarfynach** 'bridge over the river Mynach' (**mynach** 'monk'). This bridge near **Aberystwyth** appears in an ancient folktale:

> *An old woman looking for her cow could see it on the opposite side of a chasm. She lamented that she could not reach her precious animal and the Devil appeared to her dressed as a monk. He promised to throw a bridge across in return for the life and soul of the first living thing that passed over it. The old lady agreed and a bridge appeared. The devil begged the lady to try it out, eager to capture her soul, but she'd spotted his cloven hoof under his cassock. She slyly took a crust from her pocket and flung it across the bridge, and as her little dog ran to fetch it, she had outwitted the Devil himself.*

Another interesting name is **Pontrhydfendigaid** 'bridge of the blessed ford'. Here we can see the

element ***rhyd*** 'ford', which occurs in other place-names such as **Rhyd-ddu** 'dark ford', **Rhyduchaf** 'higher ford', **Rhyd-y-meirch** 'ford of the horses' and **Rhyd-y-wrach** 'the witch's ford'.

TOWARDS THE SEA

As a river flows into the sea, its mouth or estuary is often indicated by the element ***aber***. Aber appears at a number of beach locations such as **Aberaeron** 'mouth of the river Aeron' and **Aberystwyth** 'mouth of the river Ystwyth' with its famous university. ***Aber*** can also show us the confluence of several rivers, as in **Abertridwr** 'confluence of three streams', with the words ***tri*** 'three' and ***dŵr*** 'water', whilst another is **Abergwyngregyn** 'estuary of white shells'.

Saints and Chapels

From Corn-Marigolds to Holy Ladies

St Govan's Chapel

Churches and chapels are dotted across Wales, their religious heritage taking us back to the so-called 'age of saints' during the 5th and 6th centuries. Later history brings us to Nonconformism in the chapels of the religious revival of the 19th century.

St Gwyndaf's, Llanwrda

Llan and a cast of at least 600

You cannot fail to come across a place-name beginning in **llan**, and in early history this simply meant an enclosure. As time passed it came to mean an enclosure surrounding a church and its cemetery, and over 600 place-names in Wales are blessed with the element **llan**. Many accompany a saint's name such as **Llansannan** 'church of Sannan'. Many **llan** place-names commemorate a named Celtic saint such as Elli in **Llanelli**, whilst others link with a holy entity such as the **trindod** 'trinity' as in **Llandrindod**. Roman saints or biblical characters are remembered in **Llanfair** (Mair/Mary) and **Llanbedr** (Pedr/Peter). Compare this with **Llanddeusant** 'church of two saints', **Llantrisant** 'church of three saints' and **Llanpumsaint** 'church of five saints'.

Llanrhian Church

TRACKING TEILO IN PLACE-NAMES

In terms of saints, Teilo is a fine example: this 6th-century saint venerated in Wales and Brittany had a church dedicated to him at **Llandeilo**. Legends about Teilo include several featuring fishermen, and there is one grisly tale about him saving seven sons whose father was attempting to drown them in the river Taf (after which **Llandaf** is named) because he could not afford to feed them.

Teilo's legacy continues in the beautifully named **Llandeilo Graban** 'church of Teilo among corn-marigolds'. A fable tells of him sleeping on a mattress filled with corn-marigolds *graban*, and these flowers resulted in the name of **Cwrtygraban** 'court of farm marigolds', a farm in the adjoining parish of **Llansteffan** 'church of Steffan'. Teilo had influence further afield, and **Llandeilo Ferwallt** (**Bishopston**, 'bishop's farm') on the Gower peninsula, was the site of a farmed settlement owned by the bishops of **Llandaf,** where Merwallt may have been the abbot.

LLAN BUT NO SAINT

Llan doesn't always name a particular saint, but can take us on a journey in which we visualize a location. **Llanddulas** has a church beside the river **Dulas** which means 'black stream', yet the actual dedication of the church here is to Cynbryd.
Llanelwy is on the river **Elwy**, but the English name **St Asaph** commemorates the saint.

DEWI, PATRON SAINT OF WALES – THE WATER DRINKER

Dewi or David, has several places named after him, including the tiny Pembrokeshire city of **Tyddewi (St Davids)**, 'David's house'. In the 6th century a religious man known as *Dewi Ddyfrwr*, 'David the water drinker', settled here. His Christian community, founded in a hollow near the sea, eventually became a cathedral dedicated to Dewi/David, who achieved the status of Wales's patron saint. The city became a shrine of Christendom and place of pilgrimage, and it is said that two journeys to **St Davids** equal one to Rome.

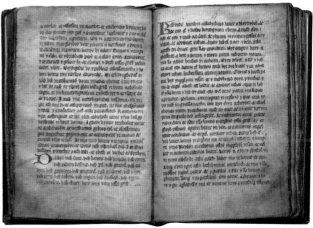

The Life of David *in the Llanstephan manuscript*

LLANDDEWI-BREFI

LONDON 211¼ M

TREGARON 3¼ M

Place-names relating to Dewi have their tales too, such as the famous story of him preaching to a crowd at the synod of **Llanddewibrefi** 'church on the river Brefi'. One of the crowd shouted, "We can't see or hear you", and the ground on which he stood is said to have risen up so that he was on a hillock, becoming visible and audible to all. **Bref** is 'bray or cry', and many believe this alludes to the noisy river or the legendary roar of Dewi accusing heretics of their sins with the voice of a braying trumpet.

LATIN AND HOLY SITES

There is plenty of Latin around – from **ecclesia** which led to **eglwys,** the Welsh for church, to **basilica** as in **Basaleg**. An **oratorium** or place for prayer led to the name **Radur** (**Radyr**), and a **desertum** or hermit's retreat to **Dyserth**. Should you see the element **ysbyty** in a place-name, it refers to a **hospitium** or lodging such as that for pilgrims at **Ysbyty Ifan**. The modern Welsh word for hospital is **ysbyty**, whereas a **martyrium** was a saint's shrine, and gave **Merthyr Tudful** its place-name.

PILGRIMS AND MONKS

Pilgrimages and monastic life figure in place-names, from chapels of ease for pilgrims such as **Capel Garmon** 'Garmon's chapel' to locations linked with priests such as **Prestatyn** 'farm of the priests', monasteries like **Llanthony Abbey**, and places of holy significance like **Holyhead**.

Capel Garmon 2
Nebo 2 ¾

Should you come across a **betws** you're almost certainly at the site of a prayer house or 'bead-house' for pilgrims. One of the most famous of these to the modern tourist is **Betws-y-coed** with its famous waterfalls. This 'prayer house in the wood' was also later known as **Llanfihangel y Betws**, Mihangel or Michael the archangel. Here, behind the altar, is the gravestone of Gruffudd ap Dafydd Goch, great-nephew of Llywelyn ap Gruffudd, Prince of Wales. A carving shows him in full armour with the inscription:

HIC JACET GRVFYD AP DAVYD GOCH: AGNVS DEI MISERE ME
(Here lies Gruffudd ap Dafydd Goch: May the lamb of God have mercy upon me)

Remains of the Chapel of St Non

We cannot examine chapels without looking at the element **capel**, which appears in at least twenty place-names across Wales, from that named after Cynon in **Capel Cynon** to **Capel Garmon**, connected to a chapel of ease serving Llanrwst. **Capel** also refers to chapels established during the 19th century such as **Capel Seion**, so when you come across a place-name with **capel** in it, remember it could be medieval *or* modern.

Bethlehem in Wales

Wales has its very own **Bethlehem**, site of a chapel built in 1800 near **Bancyfedwen** 'bank of the birch tree'. People still come here today in order to post Christmas cards with the hamlet's postmark. It compares with many place-names bearing the Biblical names of chapels of the Nonconformist revival such as **Bethel**, **Beulah**, **Hebron**, **Nebo** and **Carmel**. These imposing buildings were the visual and spiritual focus for their communities.

Not just about men

Holy places are not just about men though. Mair/Mary is commemorated in many places named **Llanfair**, such as **Llanfair Dyffryn Clwyd** 'church of Mair in the vale of Clwyd' and **Llanfairfechan** 'little church of Mary'. Female saints such as Ffraid/Bridget the Virgin appear in place-names using **Llansanffraid** in various forms in at least a dozen locations across Wales, including **Llansanffraid Glynceiriog** 'church of saint Ffraid in the valley of (the river) Ceiriog'. On **Ynys Llanddwyn** 'island of the church of Dwyn(wen)', the Welsh patron saint of lovers, Dwynwen is the source of the place-name, and the Welsh equivalent of St Valentine's day is celebrated on 25th January. **Betws Lleucu** and **Betws Gwerful Goch** also commemorate women, with Gwerful Goch commemorating the spirited redheaded lady who donated the land on which the church stands.

Celtic cross and remains of St Dwynwen's Church, Llanddwyn, Anglesey

St Ffraid's Chapel, Trearddur Bay, 1776

Y Gaer Fawr, between Lledrod and Trawsgoed

CASTLES AND FORTRESSES

MILITARY CONQUESTS AND TROUBLESOME PRINCES

Wales is a land where the silhouettes of castles enhance an engaging landscape. Famous among them are **Caernarfon** and **Harlech**, **Cydweli** (**Kidwelly**) and **Chepstow**, but these are a tiny proportion of the historic sites whose place-names bear witness to military conquest and fortification. Wales has fortified mansions and castles, along with Iron Age hillforts such as at **Caerau**. The Romans arrived in the years following AD 43, establishing military bases for legions such as at **Caerleon** 'fort of legions', and setting up a 1st-century tribal capital at **Caer-went** 'fort of Gwent'. In the west another tribal capital was established at **Caerfyrddin** (**Carmarthen**) named *Moridunum*.

You will notice the element **caer** here, meaning fort or stronghold. It features too in **Caerdydd** (**Cardiff**), Caeriw (**Carew**), Caerffili (**Caerphilly**), and in the plural in **Caerau**.

Castell Coch

1406-1424

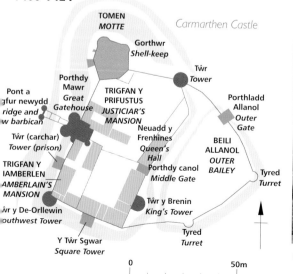

TOMEN
MOTTE

Carmarthen Castle

Gorthwr
Shell-keep

Tŵr
Tower

Porthdy
Mawr
Great
Gatehouse

TRIGFAN Y
PRIFUSTUS
JUSTICIAR'S
MANSION

Porthladd
Allanol
Outer
Gate

Pont a
gfur newydd
ridge and
w barbican

Neuadd y
Frenhines
Queen's
Hall

BEILI
ALLANOL
OUTER
BAILEY

Tŵr (carchar)
Tower (prison)

Porthdy canol
Middle Gate

Tyred
Turret

TRIGFAN Y
IAMBERLEN
AMBERLAIN'S
MANSION

Tŵr y Brenin
King's Tower

ŵr y De-Orllewin
outhwest Tower

Tyred
Turret

Y Tŵr Sgwar
Square Tower

0   50m

WARLIKE NORMANS AND HUGH THE FAT

Castles in their truest sense did not exist in Wales until the Norman barons arrived in the period following 1066. Their largest group of castles was built in the Welsh Marches, and the word March comes from the French *marche*, meaning frontier. The Marcher lordships swung in a great arc from Roman Chester to **Chepstow**. Yet Chepstow is no Norman place-name despite its Norman castle. Called **Cas-gwent** in Welsh, 'castle in Gwent', its English name originates from Old English, namely **cēap** and **stōw**, together meaning market-place.

BLOODSHED AND RED EARTH

Marcher Lords such as Hugh of Avranches, or Hugh the Fat, behaved like miniature kings. In north Wales, Hugh entrusted the task of pushing forward along the coast to his cousin Robert of Rhuddlan, who was thereafter named after the castle he built on the river Clwyd in 1073. **Rhuddlan** was a fiercely contested strategic location, and this led to much bloodshed. Its castle still stands, built of reddish stone, and the place-name means 'red bank'. The red has nothing to do with Welsh blood, as the river Clwyd at **Rhuddlan** has red earth at this point, and **rhudd** is one of the old Welsh words for red, while **glan** means bank.

Chepstow

CADWAL AND FFILI, UNKNOWN GENTLEMEN

Caerffili (**Caerphilly**), **Caerdydd** (**Cardiff**) and **Cydweli** (**Kidwelly**) were among the grandest of the Norman castles. Caerffili is the 'fort of Ffili', but Ffili's identity is unknown, and the castle adjoins a small Roman auxiliary fort. It was built by Gilbert de Clare in response to military threats by Llywelyn ap Gruffudd in this area. We discuss **Caerdydd** later, but **Cydweli**, is the 'land of Cadwal', another unknown gentleman!

BREATHING SPACE FOR TRULY WELSH CASTLES

Following the Norman Conquest Wales had some 200 years' 'breathing space' before Edward I extended his overlordship across an area in the north and west of Wales, often called *pura Wallia* in Latin, 'pure Wales'. During this time Welsh princes imitated Norman castle-builders, and castles built from stone spread through their territories at locations such as **Dinas Brân** 'fort of the raven', and **Dolbadarn** 'water-meadow of Padarn'.

Dolwyddelan 'water-meadow of Gwyddelan' in **Snowdonia** stands like a sentinel, being the mountain stronghold of Welsh princes Llywelyn ap Iorwerth and his grandson Llywelyn ap Gruffudd, who fought hard to keep Edward's forces at bay. Oddly enough, Llywelyn ap Iorwerth married Joan, daughter of the English King John

here, and despite being technically a 'royal', managed to become known as Llywelyn Fawr/Llywelyn the Great, since he spent most of his later life fighting the English crown!

Llywelyn became sole ruler of Wales in 1255, and is today sometimes called 'last true Prince of Wales'. He strengthened his grandfather's castles at **Cricieth**, **Ewloe** (a place-name derived from Old English meaning 'hill at the source of a stream') and **Dolforwyn** 'water-meadow of the maiden' high above the Severn Valley.

An imaginary depiction of a British parliament, showing Llywelyn, Prince of Wales, and Alexander, King of Scotland, sitting with Edward I

A SCORCHED MOUND OF CAPTIVES

Cricieth owes its name to the castle itself, with *crug* 'mound' and *caith* meaning 'captives'. This 'mound of captives' housed a prison on its hill, and perches on a headland surrounded by sea. The castle changed hands many times, and Owain Glyndŵr sealed its fate when his troops burned it early in the 15th century, during the last major Welsh rebellion against the English.

KING EDWARD I INVENTS 'SPEED-BUILDING'

By 1276 King Edward felt Llywelyn needed confronting. Battle commenced and the King deployed forces on a massive scale, building numerous castles very quickly. Following Llywelyn's death in battle in 1282, reputedly at **Cilmeri** 'nook of brambles', the King spared no time. He built strategic royal castles at **Caernarfon**, **Conwy** 'reed river' and **Harlech**. He also allowed trusted Marcher lords to build their own fortresses and walled towns such as that of **Dinbych** (**Denbigh**), *din* and *bych* meaning 'little fort'.

A straitjacket of Castles

From the 13th century, then, Wales was controlled by a vast straitjacket of castles, their towers never more imposing than at **Harlech**. Built on a near-vertical cliff-face, both the castle and town's place-name come from the elements **hardd** 'fine, fair' and **llech** 'rock'. It was completed in just seven years, costing King Edward the equivalent of a mere £8,190.

Just along the coast, Edward's castle at **Caernarfon** 'caer in Arfon', indirectly gave rise to the town's place-name. The *cantref* or district of Arfon took its name from its location 'ar Fôn', meaning opposite or facing **Môn (Anglesey)**. **Caernarfon** had also been the Roman stronghold *Segontium*.

King Edward's 'credit crunch'

King Edward's 'final fling' in castle-building was at **Beaumaris (Biwmares)** 'fair marsh', originating from the Norman-French words **beau** and **marais**. This royal stronghold built after 1294 lies on marshland beside the Menai Strait and was never finished, as King Edward was facing financial problems and another distraction in the form of the increasingly effective resistance of the Scots. Until it was given this name, the site was called **Cerrig y Gwyddyl** 'Irishmen's rocks'.

Harlech Castle

Denbigh Castle, town and walls

CITIES
GREAT, SMALL AND ANCIENT

Altar, Bangor Cathedral

For centuries city status has been conferred by royal charter to reflect the existence of a cathedral such as at **Bangor** and **Llanelwy** (**St Asaph**). To most people, 'city' means a large, densely populated urban area. Think again. There are a couple of Welsh cities that are no bigger than an average town or village. The most notable is **Tyddewi** (**St David's**), the smallest official city in the United Kingdom with a population of around 2000. This 'house of Dewi' is certainly the ancient ecclesiastical capital of Wales despite its size.

LLANELWY (ST ASAPH)

Describing itself as 'dinas cerdd' or 'city of music', **Llanelwy** (**St Asaph**), with its 14th-century cathedral, has a population of just over 3000 . It is said the city grew from a 6th-century monastery founded by Cyndeyrn, known as Kentigern in English. This early evangelist was, it seems, on the run from the evil anti-Christian King Morken of Strathclyde, and having visited St David went on to **St Asaph** where he founded a monastery. Here on the banks of the river Elwy he dedicated the cathedral to his disciple Bishop Asaph. **Llanelwy** means 'church on the river Elwy'.

BANGOR, DEINIOL AND WILD ANIMALS

Bangor is also among the smallest cities in the UK. Its story begins with the founding of the cathedral by the Celtic saint Deiniol in the 6th century AD. To understand the place-name, we must put Deiniol and his dangerous times into perspective. The name **Bangor** (and indeed **Bangor Is-coed** 'Bangor below the trees' **Bangor-on-Dee**) comes from the same Welsh element *bangor* meaning a type of wattle-fenced enclosure, as was originally on the site of the monastic cathedral. Such enclosures were designed to keep wild animals at bay, and the wattle fence would have been strengthened by a plaited top called the *bangor*, a term still used in Welsh agricultural life. In 545 Deiniol and Dyfrig took part in a synod with David at **Llanddewibrefi**, where David consecrated him as 'Bishop of Bangor Fawr' (*mawr* meaning 'large or great'). On his return from the synod, he founded a church at **Llanddeiniol**.

CAERDYDD (CARDIFF)

The history of **Caerdydd** (**Cardiff**), now capital city of Wales, began with a Roman fort on the site, built in AD 75. In 1091 Robert Fitzhamon began work on the castle keep within the walls of the old Roman fort. This castle has been at the heart of the city ever since. The little settlement that grew in the shadow of the castle in the Middle Ages evolved into a small town, then by the early 19th century Cardiff truly came to prominence as a major port for the transport of coal following the arrival of industry in the region.

Cardiff was made a city in 1905, and proclaimed capital in 1955. Its name means 'fort on (the river) Taf', with the first part of the name indicating the fort. The **-diff** and its later development **-dydd** are modifications of the name Taf, the river which runs directly around the castle.

SWANSEA (ABERTAWE) AND THE VIKING FORKBEARD

Swansea is a Viking city. Amateur Victorian historians penning tales about swans living by the sea were far from the truth, and 'Cyril the Swan', mascot of the Swans football team, is rather misleading! We need to look to the Viking forays on the Irish Sea during the 9th to the 11th centuries to find a meaning. So where did the so-called 'English' name **Swansea** come from, if it is English at all?

Coins marked *Swensi* and minted at **Swansea** around 1140 suggest this had been a trading-post for some time, and we know the Vikings came to raid this part of Wales. The name **Swansea** is now thought to come from *Sweyn's-ey*, **ey** being the Old Norse word for 'island'. This kind of island-naming may also be seen in place-names such as **Anglesey** and **Bardsey**, yet there is no island at **Swansea**, so why the name?

There could well have been a mini-island or raised bank at the mouth of the River Tawe which is no longer there. River landscapes change over time, and **Swansea** underwent significant estuarine changes when the docks were built during the 19th century. 'Sweyn' or 'Sveinn' could be the Viking King Sweyn Forkbeard of Denmark who was busy conquering areas of southern Britain around 1013. Could Forkbeard be the founder of Swansea? We shall never know for certain, but there can be little doubt that the Vikings gave it this name. The Welsh place-name **Abertawe** is a simpler business, being the 'mouth of the river Tawe', a river name related to Taf, Thames and Tamar.

Swansea

Newport (Casnewydd) - not so new

Newport stands on the banks of the river Usk between Cardiff and Bristol, and was granted city status in 2002. Many think it is a new development arising from the Industrial Revolution and age of canals, but it actually has a much earlier history.

Some argue the name **Newport** derives from the fact that nearby **Caerleon** 'fort of the legions' was the 'old port' on the river Usk, and that as ships became larger they could no longer navigate the river to **Caerleon**, so a new port or dock was built . This is not the case, and we need to understand a much earlier use of the word *port* here, which is more likely to mean a town or borough that was granted market rights. Old names for **Newport** before 1400 describe it as *Newborough*, and it was called *Novus Burgus* and *Nova Villa* in Latin.

If this was the 'new' place so long ago, where was the old one? The answer lies in its Welsh name, **Casnewydd**, or **Casnewydd-ar-Wysg**, to cite its full title. This means 'new castle on Usk', and refers to the 12th-century Norman castle ruins near the city centre. An even earlier motte-and-bailey castle also existed in the area of Stow Hill not far from St Woolos Cathedral.

The river Usk at **Newport** has always proved an attractive place to make a home. Bronze Age fishermen settled at its fertile estuary, then the Celtic Silures established hillforts here. Romans and Normans added to the town's importance, so eventually this 'new town' became **Newport**, and was granted a charter by the Earl of Stafford in 1385. A second charter establishing the right of the town to run its own market and commerce followed in 1426, and this brings us back nicely to our discussion of the word *port*. Place-names are not always as obvious as they seem!

Machynlleth

MACHYNLLETH, 'ANCIENT CAPITAL' OF WALES

You may wonder why this place-name appears among our cities, since **Machynlleth** is a market town. It was once much more, so perhaps deserves its place here. It was home to Owain Glyndŵr's 15th-century Welsh parliament in 1404, and many consider it Wales's smallest ancient city.
Its name is linked to its geography, as it lies on a flat, open area near the river Dyfi. This plain of the Dyfi estuary is prone to flooding, and the notion that **Machynlleth's** wider Cardigan Bay area is somehow connected to the ancient lost city of *Cantre'r Gwaelod*, or 'Lowland Hundred' is a matter for debate. The famous tale is of a dyked lowland settlement somewhere near the Dyfi estuary, and a hapless watchman called Seithenyn charged with its care during his king's wedding party. According to the legend he was drunk, resulting in the floodgates being left unguarded and the tide drowning everyone beneath the waves of Cardigan Bay. People say that at low tide you can hear the bells of the lost city, but romantic as it sounds, no one has been able to prove any connection whatsoever between the tale and the place-name **Machynlleth**.

You may know that *llaeth* is Welsh for milk, and some suggest that 'Mach' is an altered form of 'Moch', meaning pigs, linking two elements into an apocryphal happening involving naughty pigs and spilt milk. Amusing as it may sound, this is just another 'red herring', or in this case 'red piglet'. The truth is simpler by far. It is the river plain that is our clue to the place-name, and the element *ma* means plain or field. The second element is **Cynllaith**, the unknown man on whose land the settlement of 'Cynllaith's plain' was sited.

Owain Glyndŵr's Parliament

Deep Lakes and Tall Tales

Llyn Bugeilyn

Lakes in Wales present themselves in place-names in several guises. You may recognise most as place-names beginning with **Llyn** , or with **-llyn** or **-lyn** at the end of the name, such as **Cemlyn** 'curved lake'.

Llyn Tegid 'lake of Tegid' near **Bala** is Wales's largest natural lake. In it swims the *gwyniad*, a fish unique to these ancient waters, having been locked here since the lake originally formed. It is said only anglers fishing at dead of night catch the *gwyniad*, so

Llyn y Fan Fach

if you are a keen angler you need to seek moonlight and calm waters here! The lake is also commonly called Bala Lake, but the element **bala** refers to an 'isthmus or route between two lakes or areas of wet ground'. The identity of Tegid is linked to a figure in Welsh folklore called Tegid Foel ('Bald Tegid'), said to live near the lake during King Arthur's reign.

Lady of the Lake

Another lake dominated by folklore is **Llyn y Fan Fach**. The **Fan Fach** is a 'small peak' nearby. The tale concerns a cowherd who marries a magical lady of the lake. She bears him sons, brings good fortune, and a complex tale ensues whereby she disappears forever under the waters, appearing only to her sons from that day forth. Sadly, this has nothing to do with the name of the lake, meaning 'lake of the little peak' within **Bannau Sir Gaer** 'peaks of Carmarthenshire'.

The Lady of the Lake

FISH TRAPS AND RESERVOIRS

Imagine a lake described as a fish-trap and you arrive at **Llyn Cwellyn**, named after a *cawell* 'creel, basket' or other trap used to catch fish. Since the lake is bowl-like and reminds locals of a basket, perhaps the actual shape of the lake itself is the trap. Wales is not short of lakes, but not all are natural, some being man-made reservoirs such as **Llyn Brân** 'crow's lake', **Llyn Brenig** and **Llyn Efyrnwy** (**Vyrnwy**), named after nearby rivers.

Cerrigydrudion B 4501
← Llyn Brenig 4

Mountains

Crib Nantlle

ountains provide a selection of place-names and elements in Wales, many with legends attached. However, the 'legend should not cloud the mountain' when examining its name, so we need to 'seek truth behind each peak'! The Welsh for mountain is **mynydd** (plural **mynyddoedd**). Other elements in hills and mountain ranges are explained below.

Snowdon and a giant

Where better to begin our mountain route than Wales's highest peak? **Yr Wyddfa** (**Snowdon**) dominates the area known as **Eryri** (**Snowdonia**). Within this national park are several mountain ranges, with 15 peaks over 900 metres. The precipitous heights here were used to train the British team that conquered Everest in 1953. The highest point of **Eryri** is **Yr Wyddfa** at 1,085 metres. Some say **Eryri** means land of eagles, connecting it to the Welsh **eryr** 'eagles', but the masculine word

Rhita Gawr the giant

eryri means 'highland'. So don't confuse **Eryri** with **Eryrys**, the village overlooking Afon Alun, whose name really does mean 'flock of eagles'.

So where does this leave **Snowdonia**? This is 'the area around Snowdon' and **Snowdonia** is a 13th-century latinization, having only been used extensively since the 19th century when tourism needed a name to describe the area around the peak. **Snowdon** has Old English connections and means 'snow hill', whereas **Yr Wyddfa**, the Welsh name for the mountain, means 'the prominent place'. It is linked to the legendary giant Rhita Gawr, allegedly killed by King Arthur and said to be buried in a cairn called Gwyddfa Rhita on the summit.

Wales is also home to mountains known as **carnedd**, 'cairn', including those named after Welsh princes Dafydd ap Llywelyn and his father Llywelyn ap Iorwerth. The twin peaks of **Carnedd Dafydd** and **Carnedd Llywelyn** commemorate them and are often referred to together as **Y Carneddau** 'the cairns'.

SNOWDON, YR WYDDFA Caern SH6054

'snow hill', 'the prominent place', OE *snāw*, OE *dūn*, W *yr*, *gwyddfa*. *Snawdune* 1095, *Snaudune* c.1191, *Snaudon* 1284, *Snowdon* 1341; *Weddua vaur* 1284, *wedua vaur* 13cent.(14cent.), *Moel y Wyddfa* c.1450, *the Withvay or Snoyden Hill* 1533

Both names characterise the mountain as being visible from considerable distances and likely to be snow-covered. The form *capud wedua vaur* 13cent. (14cent.) is probably a L rendering of 'Pen yr Wyddfa Fawr'. *gwyddfa* here is 'height, eminence, promontory' (from *gŵydd* 'presence, sight' and thus 'prominent', *-ma* 'place'), probably the same el. as in Yr Wyddgrug (q.v.). It occurs in several hill names, leading to this, the highest mountain in Wales, being described occasionally as Yr Wyddfa Fawr (*mawr* 'big'). The els *gŵydd* and *gwyddfa* also developed the meaning 'burial mound, memorial cairn, tumulus' (probably from the location of such cairns on prominent hills) and this meaning has been attributed to Yr Wyddfa, with popular association with a legendary giant R(h)ita Gawr (*cawr* 'giant') reputedly buried under the large cairn at the summit. The var. Y Wyddfa results from -ŵ- > -wŷ- colloquially from an early period.

MYNYDD AND MOEL – MOUNTAINS AND BARE HILLS

Mynydd is widespread. Take **Mynydd Epynt** 'mountain crossed by a horse-path', and **Mynydd Hiraethog**. *Hiraeth* is Welsh for longing or homesickness, but this has little bearing on the name, which refers to gorse **aith** or **eithin**. Some place-names are easier to interpret, such as **Mynydd Isa** 'lower mountain'. Hills can be bare places, and early names reflect this with the element **moel** indicating a barren peak or hilltop . **Moel Siabod** defies explanation, although most say that Siabod means 'scabbed', because of its lichen-encrusted rocks, while others link it to the word 'jabot', meaning 'frill'. Another perplexing name is **Moel Famau** or **Fama**, in which the word 'Fama(u)' has been taken to mean mothers or mother goddesses, but documentary evidence reveals it to be a personal name Mama. Less complicated are **Moel Sych** 'dry bare hill' and **Y Moelwyn** 'the white bare hill'.

KING BRYCHAN AND WARNING FIRES

Further south lie the **Brecon Beacons**, or **Bannau Brycheiniog**, and we need to look towards Brecon to unlock these place-names. **Brycheiniog** means 'land of Brychan', which was home to King Brychan in the 5th century. **Bannau** are 'peaks or summits', but what about the English **beacon**? This commonly indicates a peak that lends itself to beacon fires, a dramatic name for a range that includes **Y Fan Hir** 'the long peak' and **Pen y Fan**, 'top of the peak'.

Entries under the letter C in the Welsh dictionary are fertile places for mountaineers, with elements such as **cadair**, **crug** 'hillock or cairn', **craig** 'rock or cliff', **cefn** 'ridge' and **crib** 'crest or ridge' all featuring here. **Cadair Idris** for example, suggests a hill shaped like a **cadair** 'seat or chair', and the element **cadair** occurs regularly in hilltop names indicating a fortress. As for Idris, legend tells us he was a prince or giant, with the **Cadair** being his fortified mountain seat.

Cadair Idris

A Portrait of the Sea

Tenby

Tides have carved the Welsh coastline, bringing saints and invaders in their wake. They have been useful in terms of industry, their waters bearing vessels carrying cargoes such as slate and coal in the 19th century and bananas in modern times. For example **Milford Haven**, once a Viking settlement (see our Viking section), is one of the biggest natural harbours in Europe, essential to the development of oil refining. **Tenby**'s Welsh name of **Dinbych-y-pysgod** gives us an insight into its importance for the fishing industry, being 'little fort of the fish'.

Harbours are about access for goods or settlers, and **port** and **porth** are the elements often seen around them. **Porth** is a 'cove, bay or ferry' as in **Aber-porth**, **Borth** and **Port Eynon. Porth-cawl** has food at its heart. **Cawl** is a hearty soup often called our national dish, with **cawl** referring to cabbage. Stories tell of a port where sailors were welcomed home with bowls of cawl, but the meaning lies in the shores of the bay, for cawl in this place-name probably refers to cole or sea-kale which could be collected here for food or cultivation. **Port** can be a port or harbour such as **Burry Port** 'port on the Burry estuary', **Porth Tywyn** 'bay of the sand dune'. Other examples of **port** are **Porth-gain** 'fair bay' and **Porth Neigwl** 'bay of Neigwl' – an unknown person, the English name being **Hell's Mouth.**

Beach resorts at **Rhyl** and **Prestatyn** are a surprise in terms of coastal place-names, with no obvious connection to coastal elements such as **aber**, **traeth** 'beach' and so forth. Rhyl presents a long, flat landscape for some distance, yet **Y Rhyl** means 'the hill', mixing the Welsh **yr** with the Old English '**hyll**'. There may have been raised dry ground amidst marshland here, or even a man-made garrisoned fort. Perhaps an English motte acting as an outpost to nearby Rhuddlan castle was sited here, or a raised fort guarding the estuary of the river Clwyd many centuries ago. If it did, it has been lost beneath the sand dunes a long time ago.

Along the coast remains of Roman baths at **Prestatyn** have no connection to this place-name, despite claims to the contrary. **Prestatyn** takes us back to Old English roots, and the fairly common occurrence of farm settlements that supported or were run by priests. If we add the Old English **prēosta** to **tūn**, we have our 'farm of the priests', and in England, such a name usually ended up as **Preston.**

Sunken forest at Borth

VIKINGS AND LONGBOATS

Milford Haven

If we look at the impact of the sea on place-names in Wales we soon encounter the influence of the Vikings. Our islands and coastal settlements bear witness to their skill as seamen. We've already touched on **Milford Haven**, and whereas many think it was named after a person involved in the establishment of the new town in 1790, it is a Viking name consisting of Old Norse words. Vikings came from a land of fjords, and when they arrived here they found this 'estuary of the two Cleddau rivers' or **Aberdaugleddau** in Welsh. They named it **Milford Haven,** meaning 'harbour of the fjord by the sandbank'.

WORMS, SNAKES AND DRAGONS

As Vikings plundered their way along the coast, their view of the land inspired them. Their word for large snake, **ormr** gave rise to the **Great Orme** near **Llandudno,** whereas its Welsh name **Gogarth** 'terrace' is at least as early as 1283. On the Gower peninsula, the **Worm's Head** has been connected with longboat prows, but here we must take care, for although the Vikings were active in this area, the Old English word for snake, namely **wyrm**, is our port of call. This long, narrow neck of land culminating in a crag looks like a giant serpent en route to the sea. The Welsh name is **Penrhyn Gŵyr** 'promontory of Gŵyr', 'the Gower peninsula'.

VIKING ISLANDS

We have already mentioned the Old Norse word **ey**, 'island', and its role in the name **Swansea**; when we consider the islands around the Welsh coastline, we can see that Vikings played a vital role in the development of their names.

Anglesey 'Ongull's island', **Bardsey** 'Barðr's island' and **Caldey** 'cold island' all bear witness to this heritage, whereas corresponding Welsh place-names **Ynys Môn** 'island of Môn', **Ynys Enlli** 'isle of strong current' or '**enllif**' and **Ynys Bŷr** 'Pŷr's island' (Pŷr being a person unknown) bear no connection at all to the Norse. **Caldey** and **Ynys Enlli** are considered important places of pilgrimage even today, with the monks of Caldey Abbey still in residence. Christians make the two-mile journey across the sea to Enlli too, where many holy men are buried. Folklore maintains that Enlli is the site of

Myrddin or Merlin's retirement from the world of men, where he lies in enchanted sleep awaiting the reappearance of King Arthur.

Below are a few more Viking place-names along with their Welsh names:

- **Flatholm**, Old Norse for 'island of the fleet' and a base for the Viking fleet. In Welsh **Ynys Echni**, perhaps island of Saint Echnus.
- **Fishguard**, Old Norse *fiskr* and *garðr*, a 'yard for catching and/or keeping fish'. The Welsh **Abergwaun** is 'mouth of the river Gwaun'.
- **The Skerries**, Old Norse 'the rocks', **Ynysoedd y Moelrhoniaid** 'islands of the seals' in Welsh.
- **Grassholm**, Old Norse 'grass island', **Gwales** 'place of refuge' in Welsh.
- **Skokholm**, Old Norse 'island of the sound'.
- **Skomer**, Old Norse 'cleft island'.
- **North Stack, South Stack, Stackpole** the Old Norse element *stakkr*, 'stack, rock in the sea'.
- **Tusker Rock**, 'projecting reef' and not elephant- or boar-shaped rocks.
- **Priestholm**, Old Norse 'priest's island', yet here someone got there before the Vikings, as this island, known in Welsh as **Ynys Seiriol**, was the site of a 6th-century church established by Cynlas for his brother Seiriol. An even earlier name for it is **Ynys Lannog** or **Glannog's Island**, and, much later, colonies of puffins gave it the popular name of **Puffin Island**.

Bardsey Island

INDUSTRIAL HERITAGE

Dowlais Ironworks by George Childs

Industry in Wales has involved coal, iron, slate, copper and lead. Add to these our use of the coast and canals, and a complex picture of docks, mills, mines, and roads emerges. Agriculture is probably our oldest industry, and we discuss it in a separate section.

Mining is closely associated with the south Wales valleys, and may conjure images of mineshafts and gruelling working conditions. **Treherbert** belonged to the family of the second Marquess of Bute, whose trustees coined the name **Treherbert** 'Herbert's town' after the first Bute Merthyr shaft was opened around 1851. Herbert was a favourite family name, and such was their power that it became the place-name for the industrial settlement near the mine. Nearby at **Treharris** 'Harris's town', a bleak picture emerges of the life of mine workers, as this place was originally simply known as 'The Huts', developed after the sinking of the Harris Navigation Colliery in 1872. It later became the infamous Deep Navigation Pit, and the Quaker Frederick William Harris was the main shareholder in this pit.

One of Wales's most famous

Christopher Rice Mansel Talbot

industrial names is **Rhondda.** Although its industrial heritage is clear, and its name is used for a string of industrial villages, **Rhondda** means 'noisy' with reference to its river, with no connection to mining. Here the *rhoddni* 'noisy river' became *rhonddi* and **Rhondda. Treforys** (**Morriston**), still famous for its male voice choir, is the 'town of Morris', and in 1768 Sir John Morris of Clasemont started a company which included copperworks, building housing for employees initially at Morris Castle on Graig Trewyddfa. The arrival of canals meant that **Port Tennant** emerged in 1824, named after George Tennant who built the canal linking the Tawe and **Swansea** docks.

Tremadoc, and then he set about his grand plan – a harbour fit for export on a massive scale. The marsh and shore of **Traeth Mawr** 'great strand' provided this opportunity, which Maddocks enclosed with an embankment called the Cob in 1821. By 1824 he had built his harbour and a larger village at **Portmadoc** to accompany it. His name lives on here, and legends of the Welsh adventurer Madog, said to have discovered America and returned to be buried here, may have influenced the cymricized versions **Tremadog** and **Porthmadog,** but any other connection to this figure is at best folklore.

At **Y Felinheli**, the place-name indicates a 'tidal mill'. Whenever *melin* appears in a place-name, a mill of some kind is or was nearby. At **Blackmill** the Welsh name is more dramatic, with the Welsh **Melin Ifan Ddu** meaning 'mill of Ifan the black', a swarthy or black-haired chap whose name survives in nearby **Mynydd Ifan Ddu** and **Dolau Ifan Ddu**. To have a mill, mountain and meadow named after him as early as 1584 must surely have meant Ifan was a force to be reckoned with!

INDUSTRIALISTS AND POLITICIANS – MEN OF VISION AND POWER

The industrial town of **Port Talbot** with its skyline of cooling towers commemorates Christopher Rice Mansel Talbot of Penrice Castle, industrialist and politician. In 1835 the development of a new harbour at Aberafan was begun by the Aberavon Harbour Company, later renamed the Port Talbot Company in recognition of Talbot's co-operation. He understood the need for political power as well as wealth, and became a Member of Parliament in 1830, retaining his seat until his death.

At **Porthmadog** a man of vision took centre stage. Between 1800 and his death in 1828 William Alexander Maddocks, Member of Parliament for Boston in Lincolnshire decided to make money out of exporting slate from the quarries of **Blaenau Ffestiniog** ('territory of Ffestin' near the quarry area). His first task was to develop the village of

---

FELINHELI, Y Caern SH5267
'the tidal mill', *y, melin, heli*
Porth Aber Bwll or Melin heli 1822, *Felin-hely* 1838
There are several tidal mills on the Menai Strait. During the late 18cent., the Dinorwig quarries built an extensive harbour for the export of slate, transported to the quay on a purpose-built narrow gauge railway (1824-5). It was this industrial expansion which gave Y Felinheli the alternative name of Port Dinorwig or Port Dinorwic (*port of Dinorwic* 1851, *Port Dinorwig* 1859, *Port Dinorwic* 1891). The demise of the slate industry (with the last export from Port Dinorwig in 1941) and the development of the harbour for recreational sailing have recently caused the community to deem the name Port Dinorwig redundant.

Coleg Sir Gâr
Canolfan Dysgu
Ammanford
Learning Centre

FARMS, MEADOWS, VALLEYS, AND FORESTS

Water meadow, Vale of Neath

FROM ALPINE GRAZING SYSTEMS TO FAT LADIES

Agriculture has always been at the heart of Wales, which, like European Alpine regions, abides by climate when caring for livestock. The transhumance system has been at work here for centuries, and just as in Switzerland, the highland pastures of the **hafod** 'summer abode' were replaced by the lowland shelter of the **hendref** or 'winter dwelling' for cattle and sheep. These two words will often be seen in the names of farms or places such as **Hafod Elwy** and **Hendre**.

Many names ending in **-ton**, from the the Old English element **tūn** meaning 'farm, settlement or homestead' lead us to place-names such as **Halton**, **Halghton** or **Halchdyn** 'farm on a spur or raised ground between two rivers', whereas in **Broughton** (**Brychdyn**) we have a 'farm by a brook'. The Welsh **tref** has a similar meaning to **-ton** and **town**, and is frequently substituted as in **Letterston** (**Treletert**) 'Letard's farm', and in our previous industrial examples of **Morriston** (**Treforys**). We also see **tref** in examples such as **Trefgarn** 'farm by a rock' and **Tregeiriog** 'farm on (the river) Ceiriog'.

On a lighter note is the name **Plwmp**. Local legend has it that the place is named after a tendency to plumpness in local ladies, but this is a wicked lie! The name first appeared at the end of the 19th century and means 'pump'. Somehow an 'intrusive l' sneaked into the name, which originated in a farm on the crossroads that had a village pump or **pwmp** providing water for travellers and farm animals on the turnpike road.

WATER MEADOWS

At **Sketty** (**Sgeti**) in Swansea, you should forget the streets and remember this was once **Ynys Ceti** 'water-meadow of Ceti', truncated as **Sgeti**. Water-meadows continue with the element **dôl**. At **Dolgellau** we have a 'water-meadow of cells' at the confluence of the rivers Wnion and Aran. There may have been monks' cells or even booths for use by merchants here. We should also look at the word for field or enclosed land in Welsh, namely **cae**, which occurs in many farm and field names such as **Caeathro** 'teacher's field' where the teacher may have been a highly-regarded local man.

The Old English element **feld** 'open land, arable or pasture land' leads us to place-names such as **Bettisfield** 'Bēda's field'.

VALLEYS DELLS AND AN ANCIENT ABBEY

Seeking valleys is not difficult in place-names.**Cwm** indicates a bowl-shaped valley, **dyffryn** a wider valley, and **glyn** a dell or dingle. **Cwm Rhondda** is one of the best-known examples simply because it became the name of a hymn-tune, but there are

CAEATHRO   Caern SH5061

'teacher's field', *cae*, *athro*

Kay yr athro 1558, *Caer Athro* 1770, *Cae Athro* 1761

The *athro* has not been identified earlier in person or in role. He need not have been associated with a school but could have been an educated man renowned for his erudition and local influence or widely regarded as a bardic or music teacher. One intriguing suggestion is that the name refers to a descendant of a 14cent. *yr Athro* whose daughter (*merch*) Gwenllian *mergh Erathro* appeared in court in Caernarfon in 1364.

many others, and **cwm** can appear elsewhere in a name too, such as in in **Llangwm** 'church in the valley'.

Ystrad 'vale' is an element you cannot miss, as in **Ystradmynach** 'monk's vale'. It is often followed by the name of a river as in **Ystrad Aeron**, or a person as in **Ystradowen**. **Ystrad Fflur** has a different story to tell, and this sacred place is 'vale of the river Fflur'. Its Latin name **Strata Florida** hints at a flowery vale, and a famous monastery was founded here in 1164 at **Henfynachlog** 'old monastery'. Its remains stand today, visited by many.

GO DOWN TO THE WOODS AND GET STUCK IN A THICKET

If woods are in hilly areas you may well come across **bryn** 'hill' as in **Bryn-mawr** or **bron**, where **Bronwydd** illustrates such a 'wooded hillside'. Another indicator is the element **coed** 'trees', such as the 'burnt trees' of **Coedpoeth**. Often a specific kind of tree was indicated in place-names, such as **celyn** 'holly' in **Trecelyn** and **derwen** ' oak-tree' in **Clunderwen**. **Hollybush** and **Birchgrove** need no explanation but the Old English word **holt** as in **Holt,** suggest a wood containing a single species of tree.

At **Penrherber** you are at a woody place, an 'arbour, bower or leafy glade', whereas **Penperllenni** shows the influence of **perllan** 'orchard'. You may get stuck if you are in a **perth** or thicket, as in **Arberth** (**Narberth**), and beware the element **perthog** or you could find yourself in a place 'abounding in bushes or thickets'. Steer clear too of the 'dense grove' of **Llwyndyrys**. Ending up in a 'ditch' or on the wrong side of a **dyke** could be avoided by knowing the elements **ffos** and **clawdd**, but in the case of **Clawdd Offa**, we are referring to **Offa's Dyke** in the sense of a boundary. Parts of this earthwork may still be found with the aid of a detailed map.

Offa's Dyke

ANIMAL ANTICS

Our tour of place-names is incomplete without a look at the antics of animals, and place-names involving them are more common than you may think. Pigs emerge as *moch* in a number of locations, and **Mochdre** 'pig farm' is common. **Afon Hwch** 'sow river' occurs several times, and 'the pigs' stream' is at **Nant-y-moch** reservoir. At **Stryt-yr-hwch** this 'sow's street' may either have referred to a farm or been a derogatory name, and since it is now in an area around a minor road known as **Lôn Bwganddu** 'Blackhobgoblin Lane', we may well ask which is the more insulting of the two? The element **banw** 'piglet' or 'pig' has a role to play in the 'Aman' of **Ammanford** and **Cwmaman.**

BIRDS AND CHICKS

Rooks, crows and ravens, **brân** plural **brain**, have magical associations in Welsh folklore, and their presence in place-names indicates their importance in Celtic heritage. At **Cwmbrân** 'raven valley', **Cwmdwyfran** 'valley of two crows', and **Llys-y-frân** 'court of the raven' we have powerful images of these birds. The place-name **Boncath** means 'buzzard', and the element **ceiliog** means 'cock', as in 'cock's cross' at **Croesyceiliog**, named after a

tavern near a crossroads. A smaller relative is referred to at **Heol-y-cyw** where this 'road of the chick' may well be connected to a folk tale, and is named after a lane running through a hamlet.

DOGS, WOLVES AND A SHAGGY DOG STORY

Dogs are the order of the day at **Trecwn**, a 'dog's farm' where hunting hounds or breeding dogs were kept, but perhaps the most famous doggy place-name of them all has to be **Beddgelert**, with its associated folktale. Before analysing the name, we can safely tell you it means 'the grave of Celert'. The tale about a **bedd** 'grave' goes something like this:

Many years ago Prince Llywelyn ap Iorwerth went on a hunting trip, leaving his baby son in the charge of his faithful dog Gelert. On his return, the Prince was greeted by Gelert and noticed his muzzle was covered in blood. He realized his child was missing and, blaming the dog, attacked Gelert in rage. As the dog lay dying however, he heard a stifled cry and found his son, safe under his overturned wooden cradle. Beside the cradle lay the body of a huge wolf, killed in a fight to the death by dutiful Gelert. Gelert looked up at his beloved master in agonized confusion, licked his hand and died.

Beddgelert is certainly linked to Celert, but dog-lovers will be relieved to know that the tale has nothing to do with the place-name. Celert was a man, possibly a 6th-century saint according to some writers, but since the 16th century at least the village has been linked with this international folktale. Some say local traders were responsible for the story, which was further popularized in the 18th century when a stone was erected on the supposed site of the dog's grave. Tourists flock to this location every year, so the fascination with the dog continues.

WHEN THERE WERE WOLVES IN WALES

Wolves (**blaidd**) are a fixture in place-names such as **Bleddfa** (**Wolf's nook**), **Casblaidd** (**Wolf's Castle**) and **Wolfsdale** less than five miles away. However, we must also realize that Wolf or even de Wolf was possibly a family name in various locations across Wales.

WOLF'S CASTLE, CAS-BLAIDD Pemb SM9526

'Wolf's castle', pers.n. **Wolf**, OE *castel*

Castrum Lupi 1293, *Woolfes castell* 1588, *Wolves Castle* 1599, *Wolfes castle* 1602, *Wolfscastle* 1806

There is a motte and bailey south-east of the village. The basis for assuming the pers.n. to have been Wolf rather than the documentary L rendering Lupus is that the family name Wolf is well attested in Pemb. Here it has also been translated as W *blaidd* appearing in a *Castell Blaidd* with *castell* in its later var. *cas-*.

SANT MELANGELL AND THE HARE

Melangell was said to be daughter of Cyfwlch, a 5th-century Celtic king. Her name lives on in **Pennant Melangell** 'head of the valley of Melangell' in the Tanat Valley. It is said that Melangell lived here as a hermit, and one day the Prince of Powys came hunting. During the chase a terrified hare took refuge under her cloak. She did nothing but stand and pray, and the Prince's dogs came close to her then froze, before fleeing whilst howling in terror. Impressed by her faith and care for God's creatures, the Prince gave her the valley as a sanctuary. **Pennant Melangell** has been a place of pilgrimage for centuries, and Melangell is the Welsh patron saint of hares. There has certainly been a Christian church at this unspoilt place deep in the Berwyn Mountains for over a thousand years, and **Pennant Melangell** can be accessed only by a narrow lane from the village of **Llangynog**.

GLOSSARY OF ELEMENTS – A LIST TO HELP YOU ALONG

A selection of some elements which occur in Welsh place-names is listed below.
A full list with grammatical details may be found in the *Dictionary of the Place-Names of Wales*.

aber	estuary, river mouth, confluence	**dynn**	fortification or height	**moel**	bald, bare, barren; treeless summit
afon	river	**eglwys**	church		
allt	hill, slope, wooded slope	**erch**	mottled, dappled, dark	**morfa**	sea-marsh
am	about, around, near	**erw**	acre, plot of land, Welsh land measure	**mwyn**	mineral, ore; mine
ar	at, by, on or near			**mynach**	monk
bach	little, small	**ffordd**	road; ford	**mynydd**	mountain; hill; common unenclosed land, moorland
bae	bay	**ffos**	ditch, dyke, gutter		
bala	route between two lakes or wet areas	**ffridd**	mountain pasture, moorland; recently cleared land	**nant**	stream, brook or valley
				newydd	new
ban	summit, top, beacon pl. **bannau**	**ffrith**	see **ffridd**	**pant**	depression, hollow, dingle, bottom
bangor	wattle-fenced enclosure	**ffrwd**	swift-flowing stream; waterfall		
bedd	grave or tomb	**ffynnon**	spring or well	**parc**	enclosed land or field, park
bendigaid	blessed, sacred, holy	**garth**	mountain ridge, promontory, hill; wooded slope; woodland, uncultivated land;	**pen**	top, summit, head, headland, source, uplands
berw	foam, boiling, waterfall				
betws	chapel of ease, house of prayer			**penmaen**	rocky outcrop, cape
blaen	river source, headwater	**garw**	wild or rough	**pennant**	upland, head of valley
blaenau	uplands	**glan**	riverbank, shore, side, slope, hillside	**penrhyn**	promontory
bod	abode, dwelling, church			**pentref**	hamlet or village
bôn	root, stump, trunk	**glas**	green, verdant, blue	**pistyll**	waterfall; spring
brân	crow, rook, raven	**glo**	coal or charcoal	**poeth**	scorched, withered, parched
bre	hill, highland, brae	**glyn**	narrow valley or glen, dell or dingle	**pont**	bridge
bref	bleating, bray			**porth**	door or entrance; also cove, bay, ferry
bro	region or land	**gorsedd**	mound, hillock, knoll, tumulus		
bron	breast of a hill	**gwaun**	moor, heath, low-lying marshy ground	**pren**	tree
bryn	hill			**pump**	five
bwlch	pass or gap	**gwern**	alder trees or grove; marsh	**pwll**	pool, pit, hollow
cadair	seat, mound shaped like a seat, fort	**gwrach**	witch, crone, hag	**rhaeadr**	waterfall, cascade, torrent
		gŵydd	prominence; sight, face	**rhaglan**	rampart
cae	field or enclosed land	**gwyn**	white; blessed, light	**rhiw**	steep slope
caer	fort or stronghold	**gŵyr**	curved or bent	**rhos**	promontory; moor
cam	bent, crooked or winding	**halog**	dirty, soiled	**rhudd**	red; brown
carn	cairn, mound, tumulus, pile	**hen**	old or former	**rhyd**	ford
carnedd	cairn, tumulus, mound	**hendref**	winter dwelling or pasture	**saint**	saint
carreg	stone or rock, pl. **cerrig**	**hendy**	old house, former house or mansion	**Sais**	Englishman or anglophile
carrog	torrent or swift stream			**sarn**	causeway, paved way, stepping stones
cau	enclosed hollow	**heol**	road, street, way, also appears as **hewl**		
cefn	ridge			**stryd**	street, main road, highway
cei	quay	**hir**	long, tall	**sych**	dry
ceiliog	cock	**-iog**	land belonging to	**tafarn**	tavern, inn
celyn	holly	**-ion**	territory of	**tan**	under, below
cil	corner, angle, retreat, nook	**isaf**	lower or lowest	**teg**	fair, beautiful
clawdd	dyke, earthwork, hedge	**llan**	church, parish; enclosure or yard	**tir**	land, earth, ground, territory
clwyd	hurdle or wattle			**traeth**	beach, shore, strand
coch	red, ruddy, brown, ginger	**llannerch**	clearing or glade	**tref**	town, township; village; farmstead; settlement
coed	trees, woodland	**llawr**	low ground, floor or valley floor		
côr	sanctuary or chancel	**llech**	slate, slab of stone, rock or boulder	**tri**	three, feminine **tair**
corn	promontory, mountain-top			**trum**	crest, ridge, peak, range
cors	bog, fen or swamp	**llwyd**	grey, pale; russet or brown; muddy; holy	**trwyn**	headland, promontory; point, spur
craig	rock, boulder, stone, cliff				
croes	cross; crossroads; also **crwys**	**llwyn**	grove or bush	**twrch**	boar
crug	hillock, knoll, cairn, tumulus, pl.	**llydan**	broad or wide	**twyn**	hillock, dune, mound
	crugau, crugiau or **crugion**	**llyfn**	smooth, even, slippery	**tŷ**	house
crwn	round or circular	**llyn**	lake, pool	**tyddyn**	croft or smallholding
cwm	valley	**llys**	court, manor house, hall	**tywyn**	strand, seashore, sand-dune
cwrt	enclosure, yard, farmyard; grange, court or mansion	**lôn**	lane, road	**uchaf**	highest, uppermost, tallest
		ma	plain, field, place, spot	**uwch**	above, over, on; beyond, on the further side, higher
cymer	confluence of rivers or streams	**maen**	stone, standing stone or rock		
dâr	oak tree	**maerdy**	dairy farm or home farm	**wy¹**	bending, turning
dau	two, feminine **dwy**	**maes**	open country, level land, field	**-wy²**	territory of
derwen	oak tree	**march**	horse, stallion; great, very, large	**y, yr**	the
din	stronghold, fort or hillfort	**mawr**	large, big	**-ydd**	territory of
dinas	fort, fortress or stronghold	**melin**	mill	**yn**	in
diserth	hermitage or retreat	**melyn**	yellow	**ynys**	island; river meadow, dry ground in marsh
dôl	meadow, dale, field, pasture, pl. **dolau**	**merthyr**	shrine, church consecrated by saint's bones, sanctified cemetery		
				ysbyty	hospice or hospital, lodging house for pilgrims
du	black, black-haired, shaded	**min**	edge, border	**ystrad**	valley floor, plain, vale
dŵr	water	**moch**	pigs, swine	**ystum**	bend, curve, meander, corner
dyffryn	valley, vale, bottom				